MAX THE COOL DOODLE

RUTH AND MARK

Table of Contents

CHAPTER ONE

Maximilian Sebastian

HELLO, MY DEAR friends. My name is Maximilian Sebastian. Let me tell you something. I am a Labradoodle with ambitious goals and dreams. I know it's hard to believe that dogs have goals and dreams, but we do. I was told that I come from a long line of royalty and overachievers; therefore, I am held to a higher standard than the rest of the world. This, of course, is very stressful. My canine mother, Duchess of Berkshire, is a yellow Labrador, and my canine father, Duke of Lords, is a white Standard Poodle. So, you see, that's called a Labradoodle. Isn't that clever? Well, I think so. The name alone should tell you something!

I am a first-generation Labradoodle, so I shed a lot. My parents say my brother, Sam, and I shed enough hair in a day to make a wig for Cruella Deville. I don't know who she is, but she must be cool too.

Labradoodles are not recognized as a breed of dog by the officials at the Kennel Club of the World. Let me tell you something. This is a very powerful organization with political ties. How can a dog from royalty not be recognized? Their decision not to recognize my breed makes me a dog without a planet. I take this very seriously. It has caused me to have many troubling issues in my life. As if I don't have enough problems!

Am I or am I not a dog? I believe Shakespeare asked this very same question in the mid-1500s, although it was written a little differently. He asked, "To be or not to be? That is the question." So, you see, this type of injustice has been around for a very long time.

My problems don't stop there. If I am from royalty, why don't I have a swimming pool, for God's sake, or a fountain, for that matter! What have these humans been smoking!

I was taking a walk with my parents on a windy day, and when we passed a trash can in front of the community pool, out flew Wendy and Carl, who are paper bags. Every time I turned around I saw Wendy and Carl following me down the street. My new friends, Wendy and Carl, told me about their cool swimming pool, but they said no dogs are allowed. So, I ask, why don't I have a swimming pool?

The other clients in my therapy sessions with Dr. Siggy Frued, no relation to psychotherapist Dr. Sigmund Freud, have swimming pools and luxury convertible cars. This is proof that I am certainly not from royalty. I've asked my friend, Siggy, to talk to my parents about this whole royalty nonsense.

CHAPTER TWO

Samuel Mozart

MY ADOPTIVE PARENTS, who are human, by the way, tell me that their original plan was to adopt only one dog. This one dog is my brother, Sam. He is a purebred black Labrador Retriever, which, yes, is a breed recognized by the Kennel Club of the World. His mother is Big Mamma and his father is Easy Rider. He's in the sporting class. Let me tell you something. I'm not even classified! The audacity of it all!

CHAPTER THREE

Adoption

NOW THE EXCITEMENT begins. When I see my adoptive parents drive up in the dog-mobile, I tell my two sisters, "Stay by the house while I check these people out." After all, I am the man of the house. I walk over to the gate to greet them. Sam, the chosen one, is too busy digging a hole to sleep in!

My adoptive dad picks me up, holds me in his arms, and never puts me down during the entire visit, which lasts about two hours. I know I have them hooked by now, and I start reeling them in like a fisherman who just caught the largest marlin. I put on the cutest little puppy act. I figure this is my only chance to get out of this armpit. I am so good that I should receive an Academy Award for my performance. They look at each other and decide to adopt both me and my brother.

After my parents meet with the breeder—a tall blond lady whose name I cannot remember for the life of me—they receive the adoption papers and vaccination records.

Before we leave the breeder's house, the tall blond lady squirts something into my brother's mouth. She says this will calm him down for the ride home. This sounds very suspicious, but we run with it anyway. Well, what she didn't tell us is that my brother gets carsick!

Well, let me tell you something. On the way to our new home, my brother starts to cry. We, meaning, my adoptive mom, dad, and me, are all looking at him wondering why on earth he is crying. Then he starts scratching at the car window, kind of like, "Let me out of here, let me out of here!" scratching. Then he starts heaving, and I mean heaving big time. Like some huge demon inside of him needs to get out now!

My dad says to my mom, "Oh no. Pull the car over now!"

By then, it's too late. My brother's anxiety gets the best of him. He takes a huge dump right next to my dad, who is gagging right about now. Dad looks like he's going to vomit. Mom pulls into a gas station, while my brother continues heaving big time and heaves a projectile vomit that ends up just a few inches from my furry white head. He barely misses my head, for God's sake!

So, Dad and I are sitting in the backseat of the car with a huge pile of poop on one side and a huge pile of vomit on the other side, and we're right in the middle. Dad is still gagging, by the way. I'm looking at all of them wondering, *what were you thinking?*

Well, Mom comes to the rescue. She grabs a bunch of paper towels and cleans up the poop and vomit, but the smell, oh the smell, is still lingering. We roll down all the windows, but the smell just hangs all the way home, which seems to take forever!

This is only the first hour with my new family. So, do you see why I have issues? This is a very traumatic event in my life that I will never forget!

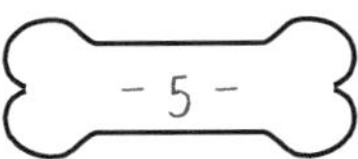

CHAPTER FOUR

Week One with My New Family

THE NEXT FEW weeks are quite hectic, to say the least. We have this cool backyard with a doggy door to go inside or outside as we please. Sam and I jump inside and outside, inside and outside, inside and outside, just to hear the sound effects of the doggy door flap going *whap, whap, whap.*

My brother, Sam, hides in the bushes, and when I walk by the bush, he pounces on me like a lion prey-ing on a gazelle. Yes, I said gazelle! Well, when he pounces on me, I go rolling head over heels. I get up, shake it off, and run after him. Dad picks me up and my little legs are going a hundred miles an hour. I say, "Put me down. Put me down. Let me get him. Let me get him!" I am ticked off!

Dad says, "You're no match for your big brother, little guy."

One day my brother and I get hold of Grandma's glasses. When my mother arrives, she yells, "Max, Sam, where's Grandma's glasses!"

Sam and I jump through the doggy door, and I have Grandma's glasses dangling from my mouth.

Mom says, "Bad dogs!"

Let me tell you something. I found the glasses. Why are we bad dogs? These types of events create a lot of conflict in my life.

CHAPTER FIVE

Walking the Dogs

MY PARENTS ENJOY taking us on five-mile walks. We're puppies, for God's sake. Our legs are short. We can't keep up. Sam and I devised a plan to teach our human parents how to take us for walks.

First, we go on a union strike if they try to take us on a walk that is over half a mile. We find a shady spot under a tree and plop down, refusing to stand up. My mom runs back home and gets the dog-mobile to pick us up.

I came up with the best idea of them all. I just stop walking in the middle of the street. I find this method to be extremely effective when a car is headed in our direction. My dad has to lift me up from the back under my front legs, and walk me upright on my hind legs across the street, while the car stops and the driver stares at us like we're a couple of morons.

Dad then says, "Max, you're a schmuck."

I love taking walks and smelling the flowers, while Sam likes to pick up big sticks and snap them in half. I guess you could say Sam is the alpha dog, and I'm the prancing dog. I have to be very observant while on dog walks, because Sam is unpredictable. Often I will be sniffing the flowers and Sam will lift his leg and pee on my head. This is very upsetting to Mom. She and Dad have to run to the bathroom and get paper towels to wipe the pee off my head; otherwise, my hair would turn yellow. Another great trick that Sam comes up with is to jump really high into the air and pull the leash out of Mom's hand so he can take off running after another dog to say hello.

One day Mom decides to take Sam and me to the park, and tells us to "stay" by this big tree.

I am thinking, *Yeah, right. We're really going to stay*.

Sam tells me, "Okay, Max, on the count of three, we take off running."

Mom walks back to the car and opens the car door, and Sam says, "One, two, three, run!"

Sam and I start running through the park, past the swing set, past the picnic tables, and way ahead of Mom. She runs after us, yelling, "Sam, Max!" I am very small at this time, so I don't run as fast as Sam. And when I stop to sniff the flowers, Mom grabs my leash. Boom, I'm captured! Mom is pulling me along with her to catch Sam. Sam is way ahead of us by now. He is standing at the gate to the baseball diamond, sniffing the grass. Mom sprints to the gate, with me right behind her, and steps on Sam's leash. When Sam tries to take off, the leash under Mom's foot stops him in his tracks. Bam, she's got us! She takes us back to the big tree, and all three of us sit down in the shade and I watch Mom guzzle down a bottle of water. That is the last time she trusts us to "stay."

CHAPTER SIX

Taking a Poop While on a Walk

THE FIRST THING a human must remember is to bring poop bags with them when they take dogs on walks. Otherwise, they will have to hike back to the spot of the almighty poop to pick it up with a poop bag.

Let me tell you something. It's a guarantee that Sam and I will take a poop and pee during a walk. I usually have trouble balancing on three legs, so I prefer to squat and pee in the middle of the sidewalk instead of on the plants that provide us oxygen. That's my excuse, anyway. It's a "Max" thing. I also like to multitask, and I can pee and walk at the same time. Mom doesn't like this because the pee gets on my leg. When I poop, I like to create a poop circle, which is very much like a crop circle. I call it the "crap circle" after Thomas Crapper, who invented the toilet. I poop, then turn, poop, then turn, and poop again, then turn. This way I create a poop circle.

Sam, on the other hand, always walks at the edge of the curb near the street and starts crying, for some odd reason, when he has to poop. Sam's preference for pooping is the poop line. His poops are lined up like a row of ducks.

My dad loves cleaning up the poop circles and the poop lines because, as he says, "This is what I live for."

CHAPTER SEVEN

Home Alone with My Brother, Sam

WHILE MY PARENTS are at work, my brother, Sam, enjoys remodeling the door frames to the garage door and back door. He leaves behind kindling wood everywhere. I just sit there and watch him go at it for hours. It's very entertaining to say the least. And, this is Sam, the good dog that my parents wanted! The purebred Labrador!

I hear the garage door opening, so I know my parents are home, and I run into the garage, thinking, *Well, you are really going to be proud of your son Sam!* They walk over to our dog run and see kindling everywhere. Not to mention mounds of cotton from the shredded doggy beds they bought for us yesterday. It looks like a tornado hit while they were gone. I can hear Mom and Dad mumbling something about how you have to be smarter than the dogs as they are sweeping up the mess. This goes on for a couple of days, by the way. The score is Dogs = 1, Humans = 0.

Now that my parents are home, they decide to let Sam and me into the family room while they get dinner ready. I can see the gleam of light in Sam's eyes as he sees the couch, wooden chairs, drywall, and door frames. You see, Sam is an artist. He creates works of art from wood, drywall, and fabric. So, while I lie on the couch shaking my head, watching Sam gnaw on the wooden spindles on the chairs, then start on the window frames, then move to the couch, I wonder what my parents will say.

I hear Mom ask Dad, "Why is it so quiet in the family room?"

They walk to the family room and see kindling, drywall, and cotton all over. Mom says, "Bad dogs!" I didn't do a darn thing. My brother is the artist, not me! Look, there's a piece of kindling hanging from his mouth! The score is Dogs = 2, Humans = 0.

I tell you, Sam is the chosen one. I'm just lying there on the couch minding my own business, trying to get a little shut-eye, and I get scolded too. There's just no justice in this world!

CHAPTER EIGHT

Door Frames and Pavers

MOM COMES UP with this brilliant idea to stop Sam's obsession with kindling and drywall. She calls Sam's gnawing and chewing an obsession. I call it his artistic nature expressing himself. My parents bring home rolls of sheet metal and pavers and get to work. They cut the sheet metal and line all the door frames with sheet metal. Then they place the pavers along the entire wall of the family room and around the couch. Mom pulls out a Sawzall and starts cutting all the wooden spindles off the chairs. Sam lies down on the floor, looking very depressed. I'm lying on the couch, watching my parents Sam-proof the family room. Now the score is Dogs = 2, Humans = 1.

Then, wouldn't you know it, Sam gets another artistic idea. He says, "I'm going to chew up the carpet.

I'm standing next to Sam and telling him, "Stop working so hard. You're making me look bad!"

Sam ignores me and gnaws and tears a big hole in the middle of the family room carpet. "Go, Sam, go. Go, Sam, go!" It's now Dogs = 3, Humans = 1.

My parents bring in more pavers and place them strategically on the carpet where Sam chewed the holes. Sam looks depressed again. He says, "My artwork gets no recognition…"

CHAPTER NINE

The Wading Pool

ONE HOT SUMMER day, Mom brings home a small wading pool for Sam and me. She fills it with water and we watch Sam dive in and splash in the pool. He then runs around the yard and dives into the pool and splashes around in the water. I am standing there watching my brother get sopping wet.

Mom asks, "Max, why don't you go in the pool?"

I say, "No way!"

Then she carries me to the side of the pool and tries to get me to go in. This isn't looking good. I refuse to go into the pool. She picks up my front paws and places them into the pool.

I think, *That's not so bad.* So I step into the water.

"This is actually pretty cool," I say.

Then, "This is really cool!" I don't know what gets into me, but I start spinning donuts in the pool and splashing around. Sam sees me and dives into the pool, knocking me over in the water. Now I'm sopping wet. I'm loving it. I get up and start spinning donuts again. Then I hop out of the pool and with a running start, I dive into it. Splash, splash, splash!

Now I'm ready to go kayaking!

Sometimes my best friend, Hot T-Rex, and I go to the beach together to chill out. Hot T-Rex got his name because the girls go wild over him. I really don't see the attraction. So he chases Neanderthals back into the caves. Big deal! Personally, I think it must be his long tail.

CHAPTER TEN

The Water Bowl

BY NOW I am so obsessed with water that when I see anything with water, I go nuts!

For instance, when I see my water bowl, I splash all the water out with my front paws.

Sam says, "Now look what you've done, doofus. We don't have any water to drink, you schmuck!"

I look at the water bowl, which is bone dry, and say, "Oh, he's right." Now I start to panic, and walk around in circles saying, "Why on earth did I do that? I couldn't control myself."

Then I hear the garage door open and I run into the garage and see my parents are home. They walk outside to the dog run and see the empty water bowl, and I hear Dad say, "Why is the water bowl empty?"

Now I must tell you, this water bowl is huge. It should not be bone dry. So, Mom fills up the water bowl, and they stand there for a minute.

I walk up to the water bowl and say, "Water, water, water!" Then I proceed to splash and swat at the water with my front paws. I can't control myself. I must splash all the water out of the water bowl.

Sam looks at me and my parents and says, "And you're wondering why the water bowl is empty." He shakes his head and walks back into the garage.

Mom tries to explain to me that this is not the wading pool. "This is your water bowl, so you have water to drink." All I hear is "Blah, blah, blah, blah, blah." I see this big water bowl and the water must be splashed. So now it's Dogs = 4. Humans = 1.

The next day my parents buy a big plastic bottle with a dish connected at the bottom of the bottle. This water bottle/bowl gadget is supposed to be dog-proof according to the professionals. You fill the big plastic bottle with water, and it drains into the dish at the bottom.

Well, Sam thinks this is his new chew toy and asks me, "How long do you think this gadget will last?"

I answer, "Maybe fifteen minutes."

He quickly chews the bottom dish and cracks the plastic bottle in five minutes. So, now we have to wait for my parents to get home before we can have any drinking water. I hear the garage door open. My parents walk to the doggy run and see the cracked bottle and the chewed-up dish. I can hear Mom asking, "What are we going to do?"

The next day Mom comes up with another brilliant idea. This whole water thing is her fault anyway. It's her fault that I enjoy splashing my paws in the water bowl, because she introduced me to the water in the wading pool.

She brings home six huge cement blocks. She places four of them on each side of the large stainless steel bowl. Yes, I said *stainless steel*. Not a plastic bowl. Plastic, I remind you, is Sam's favorite chew toy. Then she places two large blocks on top of the large stainless steel bowl, with just enough room for us to drink out of it.

When they come home from work, they find that there is still water in the bowl. It's Dogs = 4, Humans = 2.

CHAPTER ELEVEN

The Doggy Hotel

MY PARENTS AND my grandmother decide to take a vacation. They leave Sam and me at a fancy doggy hotel. This place is off-the-chart cool. There's a swimming pool with paddleboard lessons, a big yard with green grass to run around, and our room is spectacular. It has a couch, pillows, and rugs, and when Sam sees it, his eyes light up.

When we walk into this place, I walk over to the receptionist station like I own it. They are all gathering around me saying how cute and little I am. I'm getting a lot of attention for once in my life, which is pretty cool!

Sam is not so happy. Mom is trying to get him into the lobby, and he puts on the brakes. Now he's sliding across the tile. Then he gets so nervous, he takes a huge dump in the hallway and pees on the floor. I'm so embarrassed! So, I act like I don't know who he is, and I continue to get petted by the receptionists.

Once Sam and I are settled into our luxury suite, we run around and bounce off the walls. Sam shreds one pillow after another. Then he works on the rugs. There's torn-up material and stuffing everywhere. It looks like it's been snowing in our room. Then Sam gets this gleam in his eyes as he stares at the couch. I tell Sam, "Not the couch! We won't have anything to sleep on."

Of course, he ignores me. He shreds the couch, and there's foam stuffing everywhere. I'm standing there watching him pull, tug, and rip the couch to shreds. When the hotel staff come into the room to check on us, they are not pleased. They remove everything from the room.

I say, "Now you've done it, Sam. We have to sleep on the tile, you dingbat!"

Anyway, I don't get much sleep while I am there. Sam sleeps like a baby.

My parents decide to leave us at a low-budget doggy kennel the next time. When they come to pick us up, the owner tells my parents that I am no longer welcome to stay there because I bark too much, but Sam is okay. Of course this makes my parents upset, because this is a doggy kennel, and dogs bark. I tell my parents this doggy kennel is violating my First Amendment right to freedom of speech, and that is very un-American. Let me tell you something. There is no justice anymore!

Max Contemplating the Meaning of Life

WE ARE BANNED at two doggy hotels and Sam gets all the attention. I have so many problems in life. I'm so upset. I start thinking, *Well, am I a dog or not?* and *Why does Sam get all the attention?*

So, I put on my brainstorming antennas and lie on the couch.

After about ten minutes, I jump off the couch and stare into the fireplace with the glass doors, and to my surprise I see another dog in there. He's a big white scraggly-haired dog with the same brainstorming antennas that I have. This dog moves when I move, and he sits when I sit. He turns when I turn too! This dog in the fireplace is mocking me! I try to stare him down, but that doesn't work, and he stares right back. I jump back on the couch—the dog in the fireplace upsets me.

Now, it's the weekend. I'm looking out the glass slider to the backyard, and I see that dog again. He moves when I move. He turns when I turn. He sits when I sit. He's mocking me again. Then I walk over to the fireplace, and there he is again!

Mom asks, "Max, why are you staring in the fireplace?"

I answer, "There's a big white scraggly-haired dog in there. You better let him out. He's mocking me."

Mom tries to explain that I'm seeing my own reflection, but I don't believe her. There's definitely a dog in the fireplace and he's mocking me.

Mom puts me and Sam in the dog run while she goes to the grocery store. Our neighbors built a skateboard ramp right along the block wall next to the dog run, and they ride their skateboards up and down the ramp. I see their heads pop up over the wall, so I run back and forth along the wall barking at them.

Sam says, "You're acting like an idiot, Max."

I say, "I'm a guard dog, you bum!"

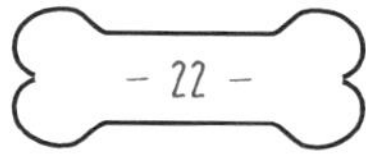

When I get tired of running back and forth along the wall, I start jumping up and down like I'm on a pogo stick, barking at the skateboarders. Boing, bark, boing, bark, boing, bark… The kids get tired of hearing me bark and seeing my head pop up over the wall, so they go back into their house.

Sam, meanwhile, is crashed out in the garage.

He says, "You make me tired just watching you."

Now I'm very tired and my tongue is hanging out of my mouth. I walk to the custom-made water-bowl holder and lap up gulps of water, then join my brother

in the garage to take a long nap. My duty as guard dog has been fulfilled.

Because of the skateboarders next door, I am obsessed with anything that has wheels, like skateboards and bicycles. I start spinning donuts when I see anything with wheels, which always gives Dad a thrill.

He says, "Stop, Max. The war is over. You won. Can you say psychotic?"

Sam just watches me spin circles in the middle of the street and tells Mom, "Do you see what I have to live with twenty-four hours a day? Max barks at Dad while he's sweeping the garage or cleaning the backyard. Dad says Max is missing a chromosome. Normal dogs have seventy-eight chromosomes, and Max is missing one. He calls Max the missing link."

CHAPTER THIRTEEN

Sam and his Magic Cloak

MOM AND SAM are very close. I don't know what he would do without her. One day I decide to eavesdrop on their private conversation.

Sam says to Mom, "You don't have to live with him twenty-four hours a day like I do."

Mom asks, "What do you mean, Sam?"

"You know I love my brother, but he gets a little wacky sometimes. For example, he pees right outside the doggy door instead of walking a few more steps to the pavers. He's just downright lazy! When Dad washes down the pee, he says, 'Max, you're a nutcase.' So, it's not just me."

I'm thinking, *He's calling me lazy! Who does he think he is calling me lazy! Dad is calling me a nutcase. I get no respect around here!*

Then Mom says, "Well, Sam, your brother is a special little dude. He's a month younger than you and that's six months in human years. He's immature."

Now I'm immature too! This is total hogwash. The pecking order in this family is ridiculous!

Mom says, "Sam, I have the perfect solution. I bought you a cloak. This is not just any old cloak. This is a magic cloak. When you put it on, you will be invisible to everyone, even your brother."

I say, "What? He gets a magic cloak! Wait until I get my paws on that dirty little snitch. I'm gonna…"

Dad walks up to me and asks, "Max, what are you doing?"

I'm caught off guard, so I let out a very loud burp and say, "Nothing. I'm just trying to catch a little shut-eye. That's all."

Dad says, "Okay. Well, let's get ready to go on a walk."

"What about Mom and Sam?" I ask.

"They're going on a walk with us."

"Okay."

Sam, my own brother, bad-mouthing me. Who does he think he is? King of England?!

CHAPTER FOURTEEN

Seeing Eye Dog School

MY BROTHER IS tired of hearing me talk about the dog in the fireplace, so he interrupts my conversation with Mom and tells her that he wants to be an artist, and that's why he remodels the furniture and drywall.

My mom asks, "What do you want to be, Max?"

"I want to be a Seeing Eye dog."

Mom says, "Okay, Max, I will enroll you at the Seeing Eye Dog School."

I'm so excited that I burp. My dream is to be a Seeing Eye dog. My classes start today, and I'm assigned to an elderly gentleman named Mr. Wiggly. My first assignment is to take Mr. Wiggly to Mickey D's. I'm really excited, so we take a walk down the street to Mickey D's.

We walk up to the counter, and the lady asks, "May I help you?"

Mr. Wiggly says, "I'll have a Big Smack, small fries, and a large Coke."

The lady gives me a worried look and says to Mr. Wiggly, "I'm sorry, but we don't have Big Smacks here. Would you like a Walloper?"

Mr. Wiggly looks irritated. "Max, I asked you to take me to Mickey D's."

I'm so embarrassed. I thought this was Mickey D's. I didn't know we were at Kingsley Burger.

Mr. Wiggly says, "Okay, Max, you failed this test."

I can't believe it. My first big day and I fail my first test.

The lady at the counter says, "Don't be so hard on the mutt."

I'm thinking, *I flunked my first day of school and now I'm a mutt! I just can't win.*

Mr. Wiggly says, "Max, take me back to the School for the Blind."

"But I'm really hungry. Can't we just eat lunch first?"

The lady at the counter says, "Yeah, why don't you feed the mutt first?"

"Stop calling me a mutt! I'm a service dog. Can't you read my vest?"

She says, "Okay. Don't get nutty on me. I'm just trying to help you out."

Mr. Wiggly says, "Okay. Give me two Wallopers, large fries, and a Coke."

I say, "Thank God. I'm starving here."

So I take Mr. Wiggly to a booth and we eat our lunch.

"Boy, this Walloper sure is juicy," I say.

"Don't get too comfy there, Max. You still have to get me back to the School for the Blind."

I say, "Don't you worry. I'll get you back safe and sound."

We finish our lunch, walk out of Kingsley Burger, and head back to the school. We're at a signal light and

I'm trying to remember if red is walk—or is it green? I'm so confused. I don't know what to do.

Mr. Wiggly asks, "What are you waiting for?"

I'm completely flustered. The light is red. I start walking Mr. Wiggly across the street. Wouldn't you know, right in the middle of the crosswalk a huge semi-truck comes barreling down the street.

I scream, "Run for your life!"

Mr. Wiggly says, "I'm blind, you fool. I can't run."

The semi-truck swerves around us and honks his horn. The driver yells, "Get out of the street before you get run over!"

We finally make it back to the Seeing Eye Dog School, and Mr. Wiggly tells me that I may want to reconsider my career options.

My first day at Seeing Eye Dog School and I failed two tests. I'm so depressed! I just don't know what to do.

CHAPTER FIFTEEN

Visits to the Animal Hospital

EVERY YEAR MY parents load Sam and me into the dog-mobile and take us to the Animal Hospital for vaccinations. My dad tricks us by telling us that we've been invited to a pool party.

So we walk into the building and I see all of these strange people, dogs, and CATS! I don't see anyone I know. Dad tricked us again. This is the Animal Hospital, and we're here for shots!

I immediately turn around and head back out the front door as quickly as possible. Dad says, "No, Max." Then he lifts me up from the back with his arms under my front legs and proceeds to walk me upright into the examination room on my hind legs. Everyone starts laughing at us.

Sam turns around to see what all the commotion is, and he looks embarrassed. He pretends that he doesn't know us.

Once we are in the exam room, the techs give us our shots and squirt something up our nose. Dad calls it nose candy.

Mom says, "Now, that wasn't so bad."

I look at her in astonishment. "Yeah, keep telling yourself that."

CHAPTER SIXTEEN

Therapy Sessions

MOM DECIDES THAT I need to get therapy because of the traumatic experience at the Seeing Eye Dog School. So, now I see a psychiatrist five days a week. His name is Dr. Siggy Frued, and he says he will be my best friend for a very long time. I'm not sure if that's a good thing or a bad thing.

My other new best friend is Sugar Bear. He drives me in his taxi to my doctor appointments. Sugar Bear came to America with a million dollars and the shirt on his back to start a taxi cab business. Sugar Bear and I are buds.

When I arrive for my appointments, Siggy always wears his Mickey Mouse ears. I walk to the therapy couch and lie down. Sig sits in a leather chair, holding his notepad.

He always starts our session by saying, "Hello, Max. How are you doing?"

"Sig, I have so many problems. Where do I start?"

"Let's start at the beginning, Max."

I start by telling Dr. Siggy that there is a dog in the fireplace that looks like my twin and I ask my parents to let him out, but they tell me it's only my reflection. "Let me tell you something. Dr. Siggy, there really is a dog in the fireplace and he mocks me. When I sit, he sits. When I move, he moves. He's mocking me."

I go on to tell Dr. Siggy about the birds. Why do the birds get to fly? Why can't I fly? I ask Mom for wings every day, but she says I will have problems landing safely.

Then, of course, I flunked out of Seeing Eye Dog School. "So, I took the old man to Kingsley Burger instead of Mickey D's. Big deal! I did get the red light confused with the green light, but we survived. The truck driver cussed me out. That was all. Then, to top things off, Dad tells me, maybe you're normal and everyone else has problems."

Dr. Siggy asks, "How does that make you feel, Max?"

"It makes me feel like a loser! That's a stupid question, Sig."

Then I tell Sig that my mom says I can try again next year. My biggest problem of all is that the Official Kennel Club of the World says that Labradoodles are not recognized as a breed of dog. "Sig, I'm a lost soul. I'm a dog without a planet. I have so many problems. My dad always calls me psychotic, which isn't good for my self-esteem. On the other hand, Sam can do no wrong. He turns chairs into kindling and has drywall for lunch, but he's sweet little Sam. This is so depressing."

Then Dr. Sig says, "Okay, Max, your session is up."

I jump off the couch. "It was nice seeing you, Siggy. See you tomorrow at the same time."

"See you tomorrow, Max."

Sugar Bear is waiting outside the building right on time like always. I jump into the taxi and say, "Hi, Sugar Bear."

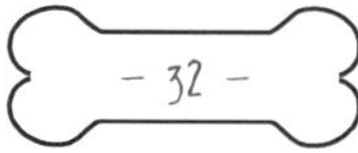

Sugar Bear says, "My friend, Max. Shall I take you home?"

"Yes, thank you, Sugar Bear."

Sugar Bear drops me off at home. I hand him a twenty and tell him to keep the change.

"Thank you, Mr. Max. See you tomorrow."

"Bye, Sugar Bear."

When I walk into the family room, Sam says, "Back so soon?"

I say, "I missed you too, Sam, NOT!"

"Well, I'm going back to sleep. Try not to disturb me."

Sometimes Sam can be so insensitive to my problems. I guess I'll worry about it tomorrow. I walk over to Sam and plop down on top of him and take a nap.

I always say that there's nothing like a little sleep to take your mind off all your problems.

"Right, Sam?"

CHAPTER SEVENTEEN

Dog Training

MOM HAD THE grand idea that she could train Sam and me how to sit, stay, lie down, and come.

I was like, "Why on earth do you want us to learn all of that?"

Mom says, "Just humor me, Max, will you?"

So Mom starts with Sam, who is much more cooperative than I am.

Mom holds a treat and says, "Sit, Sam." Sam sits right on command.

Mom says, "Good boy, Sam." Then she pets him on the top of his head and gives him a treat.

I say, "Oh my God! Sam got it on the first try!"

Now Mom walks over to me and holds the treat and says, "Sit, Max." I have no idea what she's saying.

She says it again. "Sit, Max." I stare at her with a very confused look on my face.

She says, "That's okay, Max." Then she gives me a treat anyway.

She walks over to Sam and teaches him how to lie down. "Good boy, Sam," she says and gives him a treat.

I can't believe my eyes. Sam is getting all the treats.

Mom tries again with me. "Sit, Max."

I don't know what she's saying. It sounds like "Blah, Max." I just stare at her.

Dad says, "He doesn't get it."

This goes on for about a year. Then one day, out of the blue, Mom holds a treat and says, "Sit, Max," and I actually sit.

Mom and Dad look at each other in disbelief.

Then Dad says, "He finally got it."

Mom says, "Good boy, Max." She gives me a treat.

To tell you the truth, I can't believe I finally got it either!

Now, as if learning how to sit and lie down isn't enough, Mom signs us up for dog obedience lessons to learn how to stay, come, and wait.

I say, "Who does she think I am? Einstein?"

Monday through Friday at 7:30 p.m., for two weeks, we have to go to this big pet store for our obedience lessons.

There are only three dogs at our lessons: Sam, Cookie, and me. Cookie is a Shiatzu and Cockapoo mix. She is very nice.

The instructor starts by telling our parents that we will begin with the *sit* and *down* commands. I'm thinking this is going to be a piece of cake, but there are so many people and dogs going in and out of the store, it's hard to concentrate.

Mom has Sam and he's sitting. Cookie is sitting. Dad has me. I look at him and he says, "Sit, Max."

Everyone else is sitting, so I sit.

Then we move on to the *down* command. Cookie, Sam, and I pass with flying colors. That's the end of the first day.

Our next session is more difficult. It's time for the *stay* command. This one takes longer because there are so many different smells, people, and dogs, and I have no idea what "stay" means.

The instructor takes over to show my parents how it's done. She takes us to the entrance of the store and walks me outside. She tells me to sit and stay.

Every time I get up to walk back into the store, she says, "Uh, uh. Stay, Max."

So, I give up and just sit there outside the store. Then the automatic door closes. I'm outside and everyone else is inside.

I'm looking at them like, "Hey, what's the big idea?"

The instructor opens the door and says, "I'm sorry, Max. I forgot to disable the automatic door. But you did a great job!" Then she pets me on the top of my head and gives me a treat.

Then Sam starts crying.

Oh no. He has to poop.

Sam makes a beeline to the aquarium department and takes a huge smelly dump. Dad forgot to bring poop bags, so now he's scrambling to find one before someone steps in the poop. Really, I don't know how anyone could miss that huge pile. Finally, Dad gets a poop bag from the instructor and picks up the poop. Mom grabs the deodorizer and sanitary spray, and sprays everything and wipes the floor.

The next lesson is to walk around the store and not get distracted by the other dogs and people. I go first, but I smell something and start sniffing.

The instructor takes my leash from Dad and walks me down the aisle. When I start to wander off, she yanks up on my pinch collar.

I look up at her and say, "How dare you yank my collar."

Then I sit down and won't move. Dad walks over to us and tells the instructor, "Max won't walk for you if you yank his collar."

The instructor apologizes. I give her a mean look, and I get up and walk away with my dad.

The last test of our obedience lessons is the *leave it* command. The instructor places goodies and treats on the floor and expects us to walk past the goodies without picking up one.

Cookie goes first. She walks past all the treats and on the way back, she snatches one of them.

I say, "Busted!"

Now it's my turn. I walk up and down the line of goodies and ignore every one of the treats because nothing looks or smells appealing. I am a very picky eater.

The instructor is impressed. "Very good, Max." I prance around with my head held high.

Sam, on the other hand, tries to snatch as many treats as his big mouth can hold.

The instructor takes over because Sam just doesn't get it; like I'm the only numbskull around here.

The instructor walks Sam past the treats and when Sam tries to snatch one, she says, "Uh, uh. No, Sam."

Sam stops walking and looks up at the instructor

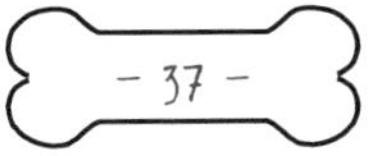

and continues walking past the treats. Then they walk back again past the treats.

I say, "Darn that Sam. He always seems to figure it out so much faster than I do."

I still come up smelling like a rose. Dad is so proud of me because he tells Mom that I did the best without any practice. Dad is gloating again. Mom and Sam practiced every day.

Finally, we are presented with our graduation certificates. I give my certificate to Dr. Siggy Frued, and he has it on his wall with a picture of me right next to it.

CHAPTER EIGHTEEN

Ninja Dog Competition

"SAM, WAKE UP. Mom's talking about enrolling us in another class. This could be catastrophic!"

"Go back to sleep, Max. You're having a nightmare!"

"No, really. Get up. She's talking to Dad about it right now."

Sam gets up and shakes his head. He walks over to the gate by the kitchen and hears our parents talking about the Ninja Dog Competition. "Oh no," he says. "She's probably enrolling us in this competition because you're always complaining about all of your problems."

"Don't blame this on me, Mr. Artist chew-up-anything-you-can-get-your-big-mouth-on."

"Shut up, Max. You're the one with all the problems."

"Okay, let's wait until Mom leaves and we can talk to Dad about this."

Sam says, "That's the only good idea you've had all day."

"If we can convince Dad we don't need any more classes that may be our only hope."

Sam walks over to the couch, jumps on it, lies down, and says, "Wake me up when Mom leaves."

"How can you sleep when our lives are in jeopardy?"

"Max, you're so dramatic. Lay down and relax."

So, I sit by the gate and listen to Mom tell Dad about the Ninja Dog Competition. Mom talks about hurdles to jump over, tubes to run through, tall pegs to run around, a rope to grab, a seesaw to hop on and off, a steep staircase to climb, and the grand finale—a long swimming pool to swim across.

This is not looking good. "I'm getting tired just *hearing* about the obstacle course. Then I hear Mom say, "There has never been a Labradoodle who has won this event."

I run over to Sam. "Wake up, you bum! There's a very difficult obstacle course they're going to make us run."

"Shut up, Max. Just let me know when Mom's gone so we can talk to Dad alone."

I go back to the gate and lie down. I am very depressed now. Then I hear Mom tell Dad that she's going to the Ninja Dog main office and will be back in an hour.

I run back over to Sam. "Get up, numb nuts, Mom's leaving."

Sam and I walk over to the gate by the kitchen, and I ask Dad calmly, "May we have a word with you?"

Dad looks at us. "Sure. What's up, boys?"

I say, "I just happened to overhear you and Mom talking about the Ninja Dog Competition. Does this have anything to do with Sam and me?"

Dad says, "Max, you shouldn't be eavesdropping."

"I wasn't eavesdropping. I have very good hearing. I can hear things a mile away."

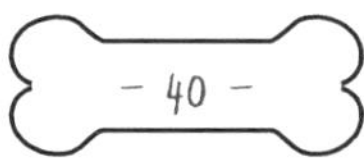

Dad asks, "Is that so?"

Sam says, "Yes, Max can hear a pin drop."

Dad says, "Okay. You've made your point. Your mom feels that this competition will help you and Sam build character and self-esteem."

My jaw drops. "But I don't want character or self-esteem. I just want to sleep all day. What about you, Sam?" Sam is in complete shock. He's speechless. I ask him again, "Do you want character and self-esteem?"

"This Ninja Dog thing is your fault, Max. You're always complaining how depressed you are and how there is no justice in the world."

"This is not my fault. Dad, can't you talk Mom out of this? Just thinking about it makes me tired," I say.

Dad says, "You know how your mom is. When she gets something in her sights, it's hard to talk her out of it."

I say, "Please try, Dad."

Sam says, "Dad, this is way over our heads."

"Yes, this is out of our league," I say.

Then we hear Mom opening the front door. Sam and I run over to the couch and pretend that we are sleeping.

We hear Mom tell Dad, "Well, I wasn't able to sign the boys up for the competition. It's been booked for months."

"What? Did I just hear the most beautiful words in the world? The competition is booked?" I say.

I give Sam a high-five and say, "That was a close call."

CHAPTER NINETEEN

Coping with My Problems

MY ANXIETY LEVEL is so high. I have so many problems. I can't count all of them on the pads of my paws. My friend Snap, moved away without saying good-bye. I still don't have a fountain or a swimming pool. I'm waiting for the wings that I ordered online. The Max-mobile with the sun roof was sold out from under my nose.

The dog in the fireplace is still mocking me. My breed is still not recognized by the World Kennel Club. So, I'm a lost dog without a planet. My dad still calls me a schmuck for peeing too close to the back door. I stick my head through the doggy door while I pee so I don't miss anything. He's a schmuck because when I'm taking a poop on our daily walks, he always asks, "Max, what are you doing?"

I answer, "What does it look like I'm doing?"

My group therapy sessions with the Crummy Puffs are stressful. There is a witch and she keeps mumbling something about Labradoodle stew, a man who thinks he is God, and a cat who wears a crown with fake diamonds.

Dr. Siggy Frued says that when I feel overwhelmed with my many problems, I should put on my bunny ears and listen to my family, who loves me just the way I am.

So, I put on my bunny ears and I suddenly realize how lucky I am to have a family who loves me, and someday my dream of becoming a Seeing Eye dog will come true.

I am also working on getting the World Kennel Club to recognize me as a breed of dog—a very *special* breed of dog.

THE END

CPSIA information can be obtained at www.ICGtesting.com
Printed in the USA
BVIW12n2012080118
504734BV00001B/1